Janet Irwin

At Home With SPANISH

OXFORD
UNIVERSITY PRESS

Introduction

The *At Home With* workbooks introduce and reinforce key numeracy and literacy concepts for primary school children. They provide lots of opportunities to develop the key skills that are the basis of primary school curriculum work. The workbooks are available in three levels: 3–5 years, 5–7 years, and 7–9 years. The activities are fun and are designed to stimulate discussion, as well as practical skills. Some children will be able to complete the activities alone, after initial discussion; others may benefit from adult support throughout. All children will enjoy rewarding themselves with a sticker when they reach the end of an activity.

Using the book

- This activity book will help children to become familiar with basic Spanish vocabulary and encourage them to speak and write real Spanish, whether or not they are already learning Spanish at school or in a club. The content of the book is linked to government teaching guidelines for Modern Languages and supports Spanish teaching in schools.
- The contents list shows you the range of topics introduced in this book. It consists of a series of 14 individual two-page units, each providing an achievable goal. Some topics are covered in two pages, while others need more space. Each double page spread can, however be enjoyed on its own, even if it forms part of a larger section.
- The first page of each two-page spread introduces the language for that topic. The second page provides a way of practising the vocabulary, and making sure your child has absorbed it.

Helping your child

- Introduce each double page as a fun new learning opportunity.
- Always talk through the work on the page and make sure your child knows what to do.
- Don't do too much at one sitting. One double page is probably enough at one time for a child's concentration span.
- Practise Spanish with your child whenever you can – for example, count things in Spanish as well as in English.
- Most importantly, give plenty of praise and encouragement. Children all learn at their own pace, but learning always works best when based on success, fun and enjoyment!

OXFORD
UNIVERSITY PRESS

Great Clarendon Street, Oxford OX2 6DP

Oxford University Press is a department of the University of Oxford.
Oxford is a registered trade mark of Oxford University Press
in the UK and in certain other countries

Text copyright © Janet Irwin 2009
Cover illustration by Bill Bolton
Inside illustrations by Becky Blake
All illustrations depicting churros by Bill Bolton

Database right Oxford University Press (maker)

First published 2009
This edition 2013

Based on 'At Home With French'

All rights reserved.

You must not circulate this book in any other binding or cover
and you must impose this same condition on any acquirer

British Library Cataloguing in Publication Data

Data available

ISBN: 978 0 19 273425 9

2 4 6 8 10 9 7 5 3 1

Printed in China

Paper used in the production of this book is a natural,
recyclable product made from wood grown in sustainable forests.
The manufacturing process conforms to the environmental
regulations of the country of origin.

CONTENTS

Page	Topic
4	Let's say 'hello'
6	Meeting friends
8	Animals
10	Fish and birds
12	Animals in the garden
14	Parents and grandparents
16	Brothers and sisters
18	My face
20	Arms and legs
22	Hands and feet
24	The baker's
26	The market
28	Going to places
30	'Please' and 'thank you'
32	Vocabulary

Let's say hello

Look at the speech bubbles.

Copy out the words. ....

Can you think what ¡Hola! means in English?

It means ....

Now look at these speech bubbles.

Copy the phrases.

....

Match the Spanish to the English.

¡Hola!   ¿Cómo estás?   Muy bien.   No muy bien.

How are you?   Not very well.   Hello.   Fine.

Let's say hello

Fill in the speech bubbles to show what these children are saying.

Meeting friends

Look at the pictures. Copy the words.

un amigo   una amiga   unos amigos

....

Write the words.

....

Sort the letters so that they say 'hello' in Spanish.

l o h a

....

6

Meeting friends

Read the sentences. Copy the Spanish.

Veo a un amigo.   I can see a friend.

....

Veo a una amiga.   I can see a friend.

....

Veo a unos amigos.   I can see some friends.

....

Who can you see? Write the sentences.

Veo a ....

Veo ....

....

Animals

Look at the pictures. Copy the words.

un perro

un gato

un conejo

....

What's in the magician's hat?

Look at the pictures and match them to the sentences.

Éste es un conejo.

Éste es un perro.

Éste es un gato.

Write sentences to say what these are.

....

8

Animals

The circled words tell us what the animals look like.

Copy these words.

un perro (pequeño)   un gato (gordo)   un conejo (grande)

....

Write in the words to say what these animals are like.

....

Draw the pictures for these animals.

un gato pequeño   un conejo gordo   un perro grande

9

Fish and birds

Look at the pictures and colour them in. Copy the words.

un pez   unos peces   un pájaro   unos pájaros

....

Write sentences to say what you can see in each picture.

Veo ....

Éste es ....

Veo ....

Éstos son ....

....

....

Fish and birds

Read the phrases and colour the pictures in blue (azul), green (verde),
red (rojo), and yellow (amarillo).

un pez azul   unos peces azules

un pez verde   unos peces verdes

un pájaro rojo   unos pájaros rojos

un pájaro amarillo   unos pájaros amarillos

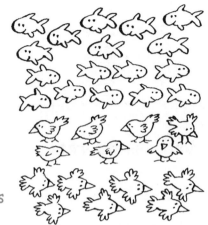

Now colour these pictures in and write the phrases for them.

....

Draw the birds and fish to match these phrases.

unos pájaros rojos   unos peces amarillos   un pájaro verde

Animals in the garden

el jardín

un gato en el jardín

Where is the cat? ....

Can you write phrases to describe these pictures?

un .... en el jardín

un .... en ....

un ....

Can you remember the Spanish for 'I see'?   It's ....

Write a sentence to say what you see in each picture.

Veo un .... en el jardín.

Veo ....

....

12

Animals in the garden
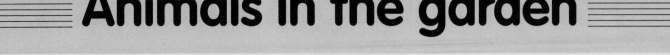

Draw the animals you might see in a garden.

Colour them red, blue, green and yellow.

What can you say in Spanish about the animals in your picture?

Try to write two sentences.

Here are some words to help you.

Veo	un gato un perro un conejo un pájaro	amarillo verde rojo azul	en el jardín.

....

....

Parents and grandparents

Look at the pictures. Copy the words.

the mother	the father	the grandmother	the grandfather

la madre	el padre	la abuela	el abuelo
....	....	....	....

Now copy these phrases.

mi madre

....

mi padre

....

mi abuela

....

mi abuelo

....

How do you say 'my' in Spanish? ....

Pretend this is your family. Label the people in the picture.

....

....

Parents and grandparents

Look at this cartoon strip. Read the bubbles.

Now fill in the bubbles in these cartoons.

Draw your family or stick in some photos.

Label your parents and grandparents in Spanish.

Brothers and sisters

Say the words. Copy them out.

the brother	the sister	the brothers	the sisters

el hermano	la hermana	los hermanos	las hermanas

....

Read and complete the sentences.

Éste es mi hermano.   Tengo un hermano.

Ésta es mi hermana.   Tengo una ....

Éstas son mis hermanas.   Tengo hermanas.

Éstos son mis hermanos.   Tengo ....

Pretend these pictures show your brothers and sisters.

Write your sentences to say what you have.

Tengo ....

....

....

Brothers and sisters

1	2	3	4	5	6
uno	dos	tres	cuatro	cinco	seis

Copy these sentences.

Tengo un hermano. Tengo dos hermanos. Tengo tres hermanas. Tengo cuatro hermanas.

....

Read the bubbles. What are these children saying?

Write the English sentences.

Tengo un hermano y una hermana.

Tengo un hermano y dos hermanas.

Soy hijo único.

....

....

Write a sentence in Spanish about your own family.

How many brothers and sisters have you got, or are you an only child?

....

....

My face

Look at the pictures. Copy the words.

 las orejas

 los ojos

 la boca

 la nariz

....

Write the words for these pictures.

....

Can you remember the word that means 'my' in Spanish?

Write the phrases.

 my mouth

....

 my nose

....

Now see how to say 'my' for things you have more than one of.

Copy the phrases.

 my ears
mis orejas

....

 my eyes
mis ojos

....

My face

Look at the pictures. Can you match the sentences to the right pictures?

Mis ojos
son negros.

Mi boca
es pequeña.

Mi nariz
es blanca.

Mis orejas
son grandes.

Draw faces to match these speech bubbles.

Mis ojos son azules.

Mis orejas son pequeñas.

Mi nariz es grande.

Mi boca es roja.

Mis ojos son amarillos.

Mis orejas son verdes.

Mi nariz es pequeña.

Mi boca es grande.

Arms and legs

Look at the pictures. Copy the words.

el brazo   los brazos   la pierna   las piernas

....

Look at the pictures. Write the sentences the children might say.

Éste es m ....

Éstos son ....

....

Can you remember the numbers in Spanish?

Write the sentences these creatures might say.

Tengo .... brazos.

Tengo .... patas.

ocho ....

....

20

Arms and legs

Copy the words that say what these animals' arms and legs are like.

Mis brazos son cortos.

....

Mis brazos son largos.

....

Mis patas son cortas.

....

Mis patas son largas.

....

What are these monsters saying about their arms and legs?

Write the sentences.

Mis .... son ....

Mis ....

Draw a monster who would say this.

Tengo tres patas cortas.

Tengo seis brazos largos.

Hands and feet

Look at the pictures.

Copy the words.

la mano

....

el pie

....

mi mano

....

mi pie

....

Now look at the pictures and sentences.

Copy the words that mean 'left' and 'right'.

Ésta es mi mano izquierda.

....

Éste es mi pie izquierdo.

....

Ésta es mi mano derecha.

....

Éste es mi pie derecho.

....

Label this picture.

mi ....

mi ....

22

Hands and feet

Look at the pictures. Copy the words.

un dedo
(de la mano)

unos dedos
(de la mano)

un dedo unos
(del pie)

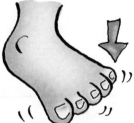

los dedos
(del pie)

....

Write the sentences for these pictures.

Tengo dos manos.

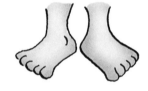

.... pies.

.... diez ....

....

Draw an animal that could say this.

Tengo tres manos y seis dedos.

Tengo cuatro pies y cuatro dedos.

The baker's

Look at the pictures. Copy the words.

la panadería

....

una barra

....

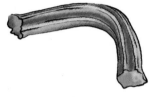

un churro

....

Look at the phrases.

una barra   unas barras

un churro   unos churros

Can you see how to say 'some' in Spanish?

some baguettes   unas ....

some churros   ....

Look at the pictures. Write the sentence.

Son barras.

Son ....

The baker's

To ask for something in Spanish, you say Quiero.

Read this sentence. Copy it out.

Quiero una barra.

....

Now fill in these speech bubbles.

Quiero dos ....

.... tres ....

Quiero .... y ....

Write the sentences to ask for these things.

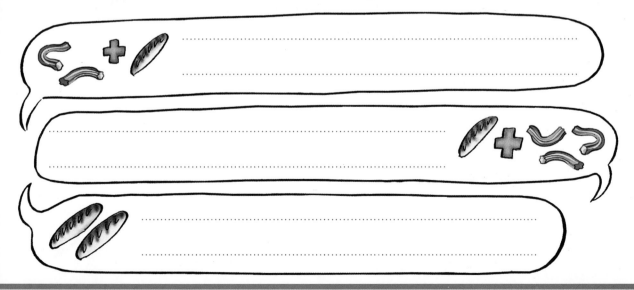

The market

Look at the pictures. Copy the words.

el mercado

....

las hortalizas

....

la fruta

....

Look at these words and pictures.

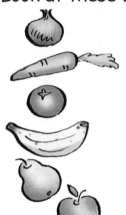

una cebolla

una zanahoria

un tomate

un plátano

una pera

una manzana

How many of what?

tres cebollas ....3 onions.............

seis zanahorias ....

dos tomates ....

cuatro plátanos ....

dos peras ....

cinco manzanas ....

Make lists of the fruit and vegetables shown.

las hortalizas	la fruta
....	....
....	....
....	....

The market

Can you remember what quiero means? It means ....

Now look at the pictures and read the text.

Quiero una manzana.

Compro una manzana.

Quiero seis zanahorias.

Compro unas zanahorias.

Quiero dos zanahorias,
una cebolla y tres tomates.

Compro unas hortalizas.

Look at the pictures. Complete the sentences.

Quiero tres ....

Compro .... plátanos.

Quiero ....

Compro ....

....
....

....

Going to places

Look at the pictures. Copy the words that mean 'to the'.

 to the baker's

a la panadería

....

 to the market

al mercado

....

Look at the pictures. Copy the words which mean 'at the'.

 at the baker's

en la panadería

....

 at the market

en el mercado

....

Look at the pictures. Write where you buy these things.

 Compro barras en la panadería.

 Compro manzanas .... mercado.

 Compro cebollas ....

 Compro ....

 ....

....

Going to places

Look at the pictures. Copy the sentences.

Voy a la panadería.

Voy ....

Voy al mercado.

Voy ....

Where will you go to buy these things? Write the sentences.

Voy .... panadería.

.... mercado.

....

....

....

....

Read these cartoon strips.

Voy a la panadería.

Voy al mercado.

Match these phrases with their meanings.

hola	por favor	gracias	adiós
please	goodbye	hello	thank you

Match these phrases with their meanings.

hello .... please ....

goodbye .... thank you ....

'Please' and 'thank you'

Fill in the words for this cartoon strip.

Look at the picture and colour it in.
What does adiós mean in Spanish?

Vocabulary

Here is a list of all the Spanish words you have met in this book.

Saying 'hello'

¡Hola!	Hello
¿Cómo estás?	How are you?
Muy bien.	Fine.
No muy bien.	Not very well.

Meeting friends

un amigo.	a (male) friend
una amiga.	a (female) friend
unos amigos.	some friends
Veo a . . .	I see/I can see . . .

Animals

un gato	a cat
un perro	a dog
un conejo	a rabbit
Éste es . . .	Here is . . .

Sizes

pequeño	small
gordo	fat
grande	big/tall
corto	short
largo	long

Fish and Birds

un pez	a fish
unos peces	(some) fish
un pájaro	a bird
unos pájaros	(some) birds

Colours

rojo	red
verde	green
azul	blue
amarillo	yellow

In the garden

el jardín	the garden
en	in
en el jardín	in the garden

Family members

la madre	the mother
el padre	the father
la abuela	the grandmother
el abuelo	the grandfather
el hermano	the brother
la hermana	the sister
mi . . .	my . . .
tengo . . .	I have/I've got . . .
y	and
Soy hijo único	I'm an only child

Numbers

uno	one
dos	two
tres	three
cuatro	four
cinco	five
seis	six
diez	ten

Face and body

las orejas	the ears
los ojos	the eyes
la boca	the mouth
la nariz	the nose
el brazo	the arm
la pierna	the leg
la pata	the animal's leg
la mano	the hand
el pie	the foot
un dedo (de la mano)	the fingers
un dedo (del pie)	the toe
izquierdo	left
derecho	right
mis . . .	my . . .
es	is
son	are

Going Shopping

la panadería	the baker's
el mercado	the market
un churro	a Spanish cake, churro
una barra	a Spanish loaf, barra
las hortalizas	vegetables
la fruta	fruit
una cebolla	an onion
una zanahoria	a carrot
un tomate	a tomato
un plátano	a banana
una pera	a pear
una manzanas	an apple
Quiero una barra . . .	I would like . . .
Compro	I buy/am buying
a la panadería	to/at the baker's
al mercado	to/at the market
Voy . . .	I go/am going . . .

Polite words

por favor	please
gracias	thank you
¡Adiós!	goodbye